SUPERBASE 22

YEOVILTON

SUPERBASE 22

YEOVILTON

Defenders of the Fleet

Mike Verier

OSPREY
AEROSPACE

ACKNOWLEDGEMENTS

Superbase Yeovilton would not have been possible without the kind permission and support of Captain Shercliff and the two Commanders (Air) who have occupied the post of 'Wings' during the compilation of this book, Cdr Benbow, and currently Cdr Hugh Clark.

The job of organizing my visits fell primarily on the shoulders of Wings' Air Staff Officer Caroline Salisbury. I am eternally grateful for her administrative and logistical skills, exercised with unflagging good humour.

The author is indebted to PO(phot) 'Mac' MacKenzie, his wife L/Wren(phot) Fiona MacKenzie and LA(phot)s Joe Mercer and Jon Garthwaite for contributing some of their superb photographs in this Superbase volume.

Special mention must be made, however, of Lt Cdr Les Port and 846 who hosted me in Norway. Their hospitality, geniality and flying ability easily surpassed anything this correspondent had previously encountered. Nor must I forget to mention the unsung heroes of CHOSC who provided the essential arctic kit and made it all happen.

Similarly, 3BAS went to extraordinary trouble to ensure that I got the shots, particular thanks here to WO Candlish and Sgt Jeff Carvell.

Lastly, Lt Cdr Steve George and his wife Roslyn; Nick Dunsford; everyone in the tower; and my incredibly understanding wife and children—thank you one and all.

Published in 1991 by Osprey Publishing Limited
59 Grosvenor Street, London W1X 9DA

© Mike Verier

British Library Cataloguing in Publication Data

Verier, Mike
    Yeovilton – (Superbase v. 22)
    1. United Kingdom. Air bases
    I. Title   II. Series
    358.4170973

ISBN 1 85532 138 6

Editor Dennis Baldry
Page design Paul Kime
Printed in Hong Kong

Front cover A pair of British Aerospace Sea Harrier FRS.1 V/STOL fighters from No 800 Sqn head back to RNAS Yeovilton after a practice bombing sortie at the Holbeach range. Leading this two-ship formation is Lieutenant Al McLaren, the only Royal Navy Reserve Sea Harrier pilot in the Fleet Air Arm. His wingman on this occasion is Lieutenant Dicky Payne, a former Lynx helicopter pilot with No 815 Sqn (*Tony Holmes*)

Back cover This fascinating line-up of naval airpower, past and present, greeted visitors to Yeovilton's Families Day in June 1990. The historic aircraft in the front row, all of which are normally on display in the FAA Museum in the background, are (right to left): Vought F4U-6 Corsair Mk 4: Armstrong Whitworth Sea Hawk FGA.6; de Havilland Sea Venom FAW.21; Douglas Skyraider AEW.2; Supermarine Scimitar F.1 and de Havilland Sea Vixen FAW.2. Back row (right to left): a pair of Sea Harrier FRS.1s; Hawker Hunter T.8M; Hunter T.7 and English Electric Canberra TT.18. Sharp eyes will spot the ex-US Marine Corps McDonnell Douglas F-4S Phantom II parked outside the Museum (*Dennis Baldry*)

Title page Two of the three Fleet Air Arm Sea Harrier squadrons deploy from their shore-base at RNAS Yeovilton to the Royal Navy's three *Invincible* class aircraft carriers as required. Lashed securely to the flight deck of HMS *Ark Royal* (RO7), this Sea Harrier FRS.1 of No 801 Sqn displays its 190 Imp gal underwing fuel tanks and two belly-mounted 30 mm Aden cannon pods (*Tony Holmes*)

Right Capt Robin Shercliff, Yeovilton's current commanding officer is well suited to the post having flown fast jets (Scimitars and Sea Vixens) as well as commando helicopters (Wessex); he also commanded HMS *Hermes*' carrier air group during the Battle of the South Atlantic, so knows better than most the capabilities of the Sea Harrier. Apart from his duties as boss of one of NATO's busiest airfields he also heads the station's determined efforts to restore St Bartholomew's—Yeovilton's 'own' church—bounded on two sides by taxiways and very dear to Fleet Air Arm hearts. More donations are needed if the bells are once more to ring without the tower falling down

For a catalogue of all books published by Osprey Aerospace please write to:

**The Marketing Department,
Octopus Illustrated Books, 1st Floor, Michelin House,
81 Fulham Road, London SW3 6RB**

Introduction

Royal Naval Air Station Yeovilton is situated in the English county of Somerset. The sheer diversity of aircraft operating from the base is simply amazing and spans almost the entire history of Naval aviation, from the Swordfish to the Sea Harrier.

What really makes Yeovilton different from other Superbases though is its singularly *British* naval character. RNAS Yeovilton is, to the Royal Navy, HMS *Heron*. Although a shore establishment it is run and organized exactly like a ship and, like a ship, it has a sense of community and robust good humour unequalled elsewhere. The Army would call it *esprit de corps* but it's more subtle than that, and to *really* understand it the outsider has to learn to speak 'pusser'.

Thus Commando Sea Kings become 'junglies' (because they're painted green and it distinguishes them from the rival 'pingers' of the anti-sub community). The Sea Harriers become SHARs, and if you want to enquire about any aircraft in general you ask about the 'cabs'. Occasionally, Jack injects his own ready wit and quite senior officers can also find themselves describing an unserviceable aircraft as having 'gone tits'.

In the half-century since Westland's chief test pilot Harald Penrose first landed in a marshy Somerset field, RNAS Yeovilton has seen many changes, hosted many famous people and aircraft, and garnered for itself an impressive list of 'firsts' and records; today you can also watch the comings and goings of this front line base from a special viewing gallery in one of the best aviation museums in the world.

If you do, spare a moment to look across the airfield. Tucked into a corner of the south side is the tiny village from which the station takes its name. The tower of its church, St Bartholomew's, is a clearly visible landmark.

St Barts has a special place in Yeovilton's affections; more than a few naval aviators have married there, and others, young men all, rest in the quiet part of the churchyard set aside for them. If ever there was a reminder of the price we pay for peace it's when the great airbase falls silent for the lone bugler.

The *last post* is, however, always followed immediately by *revellie*. With the Church no longer able to maintain it, St Barts was threatened with an inevitable decline into disrepair and collapse. Happily, its stewardship is now in the hands of the air station and restoration, funded entirely from voluntary contributions, has begun.

The 'sharp end' of naval aviation may be the carriers, but their aircraft are merely deployed to them—they *live* at Yeovilton. Like flocks of migratory birds they always return.

Home is HMS *Heron*—Superbase Yeovilton.

Right Now sadly replaced by strong, but decidedly unaesthetic, security gates, the wardroom had for many years these impressive carved examples (the other half featured a Scimitar which should indicate their date of inception). Do not be fooled by the young woman's disarming smile if you're a potential terrorist though—the rifle sling is worn in the streetwise fashion of those trained to deal with such people

Contents

1 Hawker Heritage
2 Ah! de Havilland
3 Ships and SHARs
4 Cranials, Hawks and Hot Potatoes
5 Cold Fingers and Junglies
6 HRH and other visitors
7 FRADU and the flight of the Heron

Hawker Heritage

Right This SHAR is being prepared for some minor work on the nosewheel. The aircraft is 'armed' with a Sidewinder acquisition round for use in air-to-air combat training. Of similar appearance is the ACMI (Air Combat Manoeuvering Instrumentation) pod which would be carried when deployed to instrumented ranges such as Deci and the North Sea

Below 'Cranials' are a vital and necessary piece of kit when aircraft are operating whether on land or at sea. Aside from the obvious 'hard hat' benefits, the ear defenders are essential—quiet the Harrier is not! There is a long-standing tradition of decorating one's personal cranial. Designs, as we shall see later, can get quite complex

Above The Sea Harrier's big bubble canopy is a great improvement over the RAF GR.3. With only the comforting shape of Martin-Baker's handiwork between the pilot and 360 degree vision, this one-time 'ground attack' aircraft is a combat-proven dogfighter, too

Right This Sea Harrier is about to depart for an air-to-air sortie against the Hunters of FRADU (of which more later) the small vane ahead of the windscreen is a simple weathercock to assist the pilot in judging crosswinds in the hover. The canopy may be big, but it's still a tight fit in there. The seat in question is the Mk 10 zero-zero version—essential in view of the Harrier's remarkable flight envelope—egress through the canopy being aided by the miniature detonating cord moulded into the Perspex

Left A return to Yeovilton means that the engineers can catch up on the deep maintenance not possible in the confines of a carrier. The SHAR, like Ed Heinemann's Skyhawk, doesn't need wing folding for stowage on board. The folding nose provides access to the radar 'black boxes' (*Jon Garthwaite*)

Above Lined up like knights ready for the joust, 899's SHARs await their pilots. 'DANGER—AIRCRAFT ARMED' the sign says. The Sea Harrier's Blue Fox radar has proved highly effective in combat. Its elegant nasal contours are due to be replaced by the somewhat less aesthetic lines of the radome for the Blue Vixen radar, a feature of the FRS.2 mid-life update which will enable the Sea Harrier to engage targets at beyond visual range. The large building in the background is the Fleet Air Arm Museum, and the recently extended 'History of V/STOL' gallery overlooks this very flight line. This uniquely allows study of the earliest history of vertical flight whilst the sight, sound, and aroma of the latest developments can be experienced just outside. This is very much a *living* museum

Below These pictures were taken in the summer of 1990 as the V/STOL gallery was being readied for opening. This resulted in 'Great Grandad' coming out for some air and a fresh coat of paint. Progenitor of the SHARs it proudly overlooks, this early development (P.1127) airframe is a very different machine indeed from today's complex and capable multi-role fighter

Left The overall dark grey 'low vis' scheme dates from the Falklands campaign, where the Harrier/Sidewinder combination proved deadly. Trialled and delivered during that conflict was a twin launcher for the 'Winders which doubled the aircraft's AAM armament without compromising the inboard pylons. The SHAR can carry a variety of weaponry, including iron and cluster bombs, 'smart' laser-guided munitions, and Sea Eagle air-to-surface missiles for the anti-shipping role. Also visible are the belly-mounted Aden 30 mm cannons—an essential adjunct for both air-to-air and air-to-surface combat at close ranges (*'Mac' MacKenzie*)

It's late afternoon as this SHAR hits the ramp for another launch. Being flung skywards in this way may seem drastic but is a straightforward operation for the pilot. The increased weight take-offs made possible by the ramp significantly improve the aircraft's range and payload

Above The raised cockpit gives the instructor an excellent view, but adds to the gawkiness of the two-seater on its bicycle undercarriage. This is further emphasized by the substitution of airflow strakes in place of the twin cannon

Left Next! A Sidewinder-toting Sea Harrier cranks up for its turn on the ramp

There are three Sea Harrier squadrons home-based at HMS *Heron*. No 899 NAS as the training unit is of course the most frequently seen, their distinctive winged gauntlet (dating back in its present form to the days of the Sea Vixen), being easily identifiable

Preceding pages Ignition! The Hunter's trusty Avon turbojet howls into life using the standard three-shot turbo-starter system which, by means of a miniature gas turbine and self-reduction gear and clutch, drives on the front of the main engine shaft and accelerates the engine to a self-sustaining 2000 rpm (*Dennis Baldry*)

Right Even in its two-seat form the Hunter retains its classic elegance of line. The year 1991 will see the 40th anniversary of Sir Sydney Camm's much loved design, and there is every reason to suppose that more than a few will still be around for the half-century

Above Reminiscent of a scene from San Carlos Water during the Falklands conflict in 1982, a Hunter T.7 masquerades as the 'enemy' as it swoops in between the Royal Fleet Auxiliary (RFA) *Blue Rover* and the Type 42 destroyer HMS *Birmingham*. During the course of this Basic Operational Sea Training (BOST) mission, this FRADU Hunter performed both 'attacking aircraft' and 'sea-skimming missile' attack profiles (*Tony Holmes*)

Left A flashback to an earlier age. In the late sixties and early seventies 'dayglo' was much in vogue for training aircraft. Similarly, the silver or natural metal base finishes of yore gave way to the rather smarter Light Aircraft Grey seen here. As ever the Royal Navy came up with a distinctively different scheme for their aircraft (*Fiona MacKenzie*)

Below Whilst the airframes belong to the Navy, FRADU is operated under contract by Flight Refuelling Ltd, who provide all the manpower on the ground as well as the pilots. The *rad haz* patch on this chap's cranial presumably means he can stop the oncoming Hunter by sheer willpower if necessary

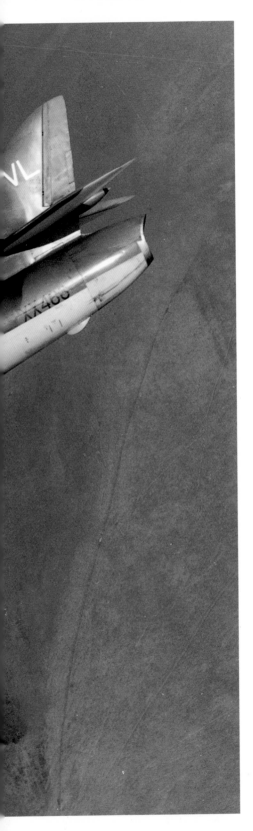

Left This shot from Yeovilton's archives clearly has a story attached to it. The aircraft is a T.7 complete with RAF colour scheme and squadron crest, but it had undoubtedly been taken onto FRADU's strength as evidenced by the nose number and 'VL' tail code (*LA(phot) Thomas*)

Above Also on the south side flight line are two T.8Ms which belong to No 899 NAS. These aircraft are fitted with a Sea Harrier-type cockpit layout and, more obviously, the Blue Fox radar nose. The T.8M enables SHAR pilots to train effectively on the Blue Fox radar system without burning expensive Sea Harrier hours. These Hunters often carry AIM-9 acquisition rounds on the outboard pylons (above which the sharp-eyed amongst you will detect the tower of Yeovilton church shimmering in the jet efflux), and are also distinguished by the 'high vis' presentation of the squadron's tail emblem

Above Nasal variations: four different types of Hunter on the line. Acquired towards the end of the fifties, 71 surplus Hunter F.4s were obtained from the RAF and converted to naval standards, emerging as GA.11s (the T.8s were converted on the production line from the basic T.7). As the Hunter will continue to serve 'for the foreseeable future', the £30,000 paid for each F.4 has proved to be very cost effective

Right In late 1990 Yeovilton still had one last Hunter in the old grey and white scheme, a nostalgic sight amongst all the toned-down schemes of the post-Falklands era

Ah! de Havilland

Hawker isn't the only great *marque* to be found at Yeovilton. The products of the de Havilland company—both the parent and its Canadian subsidiary—are also much in evidence. Heron Flight operates two Chipmunk primary trainers for Historic Flight proficiency flying and, at weekends, for glider towing. Something of an anachronism in the jet age, the 'Chippie' mixes metal and fabric construction and is not exactly overpowered. Unlike many modern 'club' types it is not viceless either and needs to be treated with the proper respect due to an old lady (this author actually did once find himself 'upside down with nothing on the clock...' but that's another story). Nevertheless it is fully aerobatic and a joy to fly

Right December 1989. Below the cloud layer it's a crisp winter day, but up here two of Heron Flight's appropriately named de Havilland D.H.114 Sea Herons practice for their last formation flight in unbroken sunshine

Above After a long and distinguished career these immaculate and elegant aircraft are finally to be replaced. First built in the mid-fifties, these airframes have seen service with operators as diverse as Nigerian Airways and Jersey Airlines before coming to the RN. Here Lt Cdr Fergus Woods and PO Blackburn bring XR441 in close for the camera

Unencumbered by armament, radar, flight refuelling probe and assorted items of naval paraphernalia, the Llandbedr Sea Vixens are probably spritely performers compared to operational FAW.2s. Powered by two Rolls-Royce 208 turbojets with a sea level static thrust rating of 11,250 lb, the Sea Vixen is capable of sustaining about 650 mph (Mach 0.94) on the level at medium altitudes

Left After the disastrous disintegration of the prototype D.H.110 during the Farnborough Air Show in 1952, de Havilland were determined to eliminate any possibility of structural failure in production aircraft. As a result the second, semi-navalized D.H.110 emerged in June 1955 as a somewhat 'overbuilt' aircraft with a greater empty weight than was strictly necessary for the design mission. Seemingly 'fettled' into shape by craftsmen, the Sea Vixen proved to be a tough aircraft which stood up reasonably well to the rigours of carrier operations

Below The dark skies which threatened the barbecues on Families Day provide a dramatic backdrop for some of the FAA Museum's aircraft. In the foreground is a Sea Vixen FAW.2 bearing the winged gauntlet motif of No 899, the last squadron to operate the aircraft in Fleet service. Compared to the FAW.1, the FAW.2 had considerably greater endurance due to the additional fuel contained in the pinion tanks formed by the overwing extensions of the tail booms and the addition of a flight refuelling probe

Ships and SHARs

HMS *Ark Royal*, somewhere in the North Sea, September 1990. The *raison d'être* of Yeovilton's Sea Harriers is of course deployment at sea with the Fleet. Without the Harrier and the carriers HMS *Invincible* and HMS *Hermes* (the latter now serves with the Indian Navy as INS *Viraat*), the UK would not have been able to mount Operation Corporate and successfully recover the Falkland Islands from Argentina in May 1982. Prior to the Falklands conflict, the Navy's fixed-wing airpower was in decline; Britain's last conventional carrier, the fourth HMS *Ark Royal*, had followed HMS *Eagle* to the breaker's yard in 1979 and her Phantoms and Buccaneers transferred to the RAF. The advent of the much smaller Invincible class 'through-deck cruiser' and the Sea Harrier was seen as a cost-effective way of maintaining a useful carrier capability; even so, HMS *Invincible* was almost sold to Australia as part of a further round of defence cuts which planned to reduce the number of RN carriers from three to two. Post-Falklands, the Navy now feels able to again talk openly about its carrier force, being reasonably confident that at last British politicians understand the need for organic naval airpower (*Jon Garthwaite*)

Above Twenty minutes since the first alarm and the sun is already well down in the west. (The gathering gloom just adds a little more to the rescuers' difficulties.) Things are now much more ordered, casualties accounted for and prioritized for medevac. One of the first people off the rapid response aircraft is the incident control officer who co-ordinates rescue activity directly from the site

Right The most seriously 'injured' are lifted directly out from the nearest landing site—reached by the rescue party after a strenuous climb up a rough track, through a hedgerow and over a ditch into the field. Paramedics brace themselves as the first aircraft leaves. The next helicopter is already orbiting to collect the stretcher cases

Above left The days are short this far north and the late afternoon sun emphasizes the wilderness below

Below left Caught against the sheer wall of a mountainside deep in shadow, this aircraft is lit up by the low sun as it turns to run down the valley. This results from observing peacetime minimum heights. In a combat situation 'lit up' is the last thing a tactical helo wants to be and the mission would be flown *much* lower

Above As we head back to Tretten the last rays of the setting sun afford an opportunity to more readily appreciate the contours of the Sea King. The HC.4 has proved a remarkably versatile and capable shifter of both soldiers and supplies. A capacious cabin and very respectable underslung load capability keeps it much in demand

Left 'Victor Juliet' again in somewhat less attractive conditions on top of a snow-laden mountain

Above Not all junglies are green. Here we formate on 'Victor Papa', which has been treated to the full temporary arctic scheme. Low level tactical flying in Norway has one overriding hazard—the wires. With no apparent thought for the needs of rotary wing aviators, the Norwegians simply take their power and communication cables by the shortest route. If this happens to be across a valley, the plethora of wires involved can form a cat's cradle to entangle the unwary. The pilots' stay in 'heads up' mode for most of the time when this type of hazard is likely to be encountered, all eyes scanning the terrain ahead

Left Having safely negotiated the valleys below our two aircraft climb towards the mountain peak

Above To get soldiers to places as inaccessible as this is difficult even for a helicopter. There's nowhere on this knife-edge ridge big enough to actually land, and the pilot will have to maintain the hover whilst everyone gets out

'Papa' finally finds a spot slightly lower down with enough room for all three wheels. The once pristine finish has suffered much from the effects of exhaust and oil generated by the turboshaft engines

Left Back in Norway the Royal Marines also use the Lynx and Gazelle aircraft of 3 Commando Brigade Air Squadron—known universally as simply '3BAS'. Tasked with support of the brigade worldwide, 3BAS lives at Yeovilton. It will come as no surprise to the reader to learn that it is a unique formation. Firstly, its aircraft are the only ones that actually 'belong' to the Royal Marines. As their role is anti-armour support, they are also unique in that they take to sea virtually un-navalized aircraft. (The Gazelle never has been navalized; the Lynx AH.1 and AH.7 are essentially 'Army' variants, very different from their web-footed relatives)

Above The nimble and attractive Gazelle is an Anglo-French design produced, as are all helicopters in the UK, by Westland Aircraft—based 'just down the road' at Yeovil. Its primary role is observation and reconnaissance, which includes spotting for artillery and Forward Air Control. It is also ideal for the rapid movement of key personnel, which is what this Gazelle is doing

Left *BAS goes hunting*—the Castle Martin FARP in South Wales is the jump-off point for a series of HELARM (anti-armour) exercises which pit the aircraft of 3BAS against tanks on manoeuvre. In this case the opposition are some German Leopard 2s

Above For the purpose of this exercise one Gazelle controls each pair of TOW-armed Lynx. The Gazelle crew have tactical control and strive to get the Lynxes into good firing positions without the 'bad guys' seeing them. At the adjudged moment the weapons helos are told to 'unmask' and engage the target. If they've got it right the Lynx will be near enough to minimize the flight time of the missile (and thus their exposure to return fire) but far enough away to keep them out of trouble. This aircraft is just settling into the Welsh grass as it waits its turn at the camouflaged fuel bowser. Note the skilfully concealed vehicle blending into the hedgerow in the background

Overleaf Returning to Yeovilton over the Bristol Channel a Gazelle escorts its pair of Lynx. All three aircraft are fitted with a roof-mounted telescopic sight for target acquisition. Prominent from this angle is the Gazelle's 'fenestron' shrouded tail rotor

Above The Lynx is also an Anglo-French design. Westland have enhanced the basic design considerably since the prototype WG.13 first flew in March 1971. A Lynx fitted with the revolutionary BERP rotor currently holds the world speed record for its class at 249.09 mph. For the time being the Royal Marines still use the Lynx AH.1 version (which the British Army have operated since 1976), along with the improved but externally almost identical Mk 7. The airframe is essentially designed for utility and endows a degree of flexibility that 3BAS finds useful. The Lynx is not a dedicated attack helicopter; (an attack variant with a new fuselage was schemed but never left the drawing board). However, armed with eight battle-proven TOW missiles and with space in the cabin for its own re-loads, the Lynx is not to be taken lightly

Right Back at Castle Martin another aircraft sits quietly in the midday sun whilst the crews brief. Still wearing the 'old standard' black and green Army paint scheme this aircraft will eventually get the 'new standard' grey and green seen on the Gazelles

Capable of carrying a small infantry squad or recon team the Lynx is occasionally used for specialized people moving. The people in question will, by the nature of their calling, wish to be deposited in remote and inaccessible places where it may not be possible for the helo to land. No matter, the Royal Marines are dab hands at abseiling, and a helicopter is as good a place to do it from as any! This of course is a training session at Yeovilton. A couple of hours' window in the fly pro is being taken full advantage of by cycling as many Marines as possible through some 'heli-abseiling'

Above Another denizen of the Museum is the Supermarine Scimitar F.1 — an aircraft which, but for the advent of the Sea Harrier, would have been the Navy's last single-seat carrier-borne fighter. The FAA received the first of its 76 Scimitars in June 1958. In addition to its powerful built-in armament of four 30 mm Aden cannon, the Scimitar was capable of carrying 96 un-guided air-to-air rockets, four Sidewinder AAMs, four Bullpup ASMs or a tactical nuclear weapon. Despite a combined 22,500 lbs of thrust from its Rolls-Royce Avon turbojets, the Scimitar was steadfastly subsonic in level flight. Although popular with its pilots, who enjoyed particularly good visibility from the cockpit, the Scimitar is mostly remembered for its copious fuel leaks — which required dustbins rather than drip trays

Left Using a curved approach technique, the Fleet Air Arm gained distinction of being the first service to operate the Vought F4U Corsair fighter-bomber at sea in World War 2, the US Navy having decided that the view over the Corsair's long snout was unacceptable when the aircraft was low, slow and nose high on the final approach. *'Never mind the deck, I couldn't even see the carrier!'* was how one American pilot put it. Featuring clipped wing tips which allowed the aircraft to fit the smaller hangar decks of British carriers, the Museum's example, KD431, is an F4U-6, designated Corsair Mk 4 in FAA service

FRADU and the flight of the Heron

Right Heron Flight is located on the south side of the airfield and probably has the most wide-ranging responsibilities of any unit on the station. Operating a single Heron and a fleet of six BAe Jetstreams, Heron Flight is the Navy's airline, ferrying passengers and small items of priority cargo speedily and efficiently. It also has the Historic Flight under its wing and acts as the Aircraft Servicing Flight (ASF) for a wide variety of visiting aircraft. The flight line is also shared with the Hunters, Falcons and Canberras of FRADU. The Jetstream seen here is the latest version to be taken on strength by the Navy; powered by American Garrett TPE331 turboprops turning British Dowty propellers, this sleek aircraft is based on the successful Jetstream 31 business and commuter airliner

Below Originally used as cargo aircraft by the American package-carrying giant Federal Express, some sixteen refurbished and re-equipped Dassault Falcon 20s are operated by Flight Refuelling Ltd on behalf of the Navy to perform target towing and electronic warfare training duties

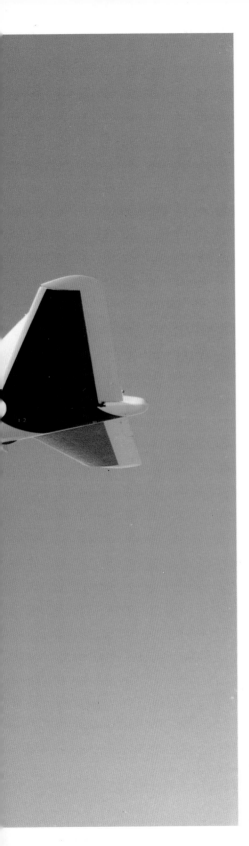

Two views of the FRADU's unmistakably marked Canberra TT.18 target towing aircraft. The Rushton target system carried under the wings is capable of simulating radar and infrared targets. Apart from the relatively minor modifications required to adapt the aircraft for target towing, this Canberra is virtually identical to the RAF B.2 bomber version which entered service in October 1950 (*'Mac' MacKenzie*)

The much-loved Fairey Swordfish is one of the few great combat aircraft which became legends in their own lifetime. First flown in prototype form in April 1934, the Swordfish was thought by many to be obsolete when World War 2 broke out five years later. But on the night of 10–11 October 1940, two waves of Swordfish from the carrier HMS *Illustrious* attacked the Italian naval base at Taranto and sank three battleships, a cruiser, two destroyers and other warships. A 'Stringbag' from HMS *Ark Royal* jammed the rudder of the German battleship *Bismarck* with a torpedo in May 1941, allowing the Navy's pursuing capital ships to catch and sink her in the North Atlantic. A large volume would be required to do justice to the other exploits of this amazing machine. Thanks to the Historic Flight, the courage of the crews who manned the Swordfish is appropriately commemorated. The white and gray camouflage scheme currently worn by the Flight's Swordfish is representative of that applied to the aircraft when it was engaged in convoy protection duties in the North Atlantic during 1944 (*'Mac' MacKenzie*)

Despite appearances, the Sea Harrier and the Fairey Firefly are not flying in
formation but travelling at different speeds. The Sea King helicopter from which
'Mac' MacKenzie took this photograph is flying flat out to prevent the formating
Firefly from stalling; it took several 'dummy runs' before the Sea Harrier and
Firefly were simultaneously positioned in 'Mac's' viewfinder. The Flight's
Firefly is an FR.5 fighter reconnaissance version originally delivered to the
Royal Australian Navy in the early fifties; a superb fund raising effort in the
wardroom of HMS *Victorious* enabled the aircraft to be transported back to the
UK for restoration to flying condition (*'Mac' MacKenzie*)